# U.S. PRESIDENTS

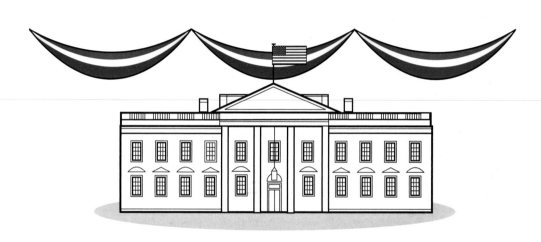

KINGFISHER
NEW YORK

# KINGFISHER
## LONDON & NEW YORK

Text and design copyright © Toucan Books Ltd. 2013, 2017
Based on an original concept by Toucan Books Ltd.
Illustrations copyright © Simon Basher 2013, 2017

Published in the United States by Kingfisher,
175 Fifth Ave., New York, NY 10010
Kingfisher is an imprint of Macmillan Children's Books, London.

Consultant: Ted Widmer

Designed and created by Basher  www.basherbooks.com
Text written by Dan Green

Dedicated to Ellen Dupont and with thanks to Hayley Burstein

Distributed in the U.S. and Canada by Macmillan,
175 Fifth Ave., New York, NY 10010

Library of Congress Cataloging-in-Publication data has been applied for.

ISBN: 978-0-7534-7319-1 (PB)
ISBN: 978-0-7534-7318-4 (HB)

Kingfisher books are available for special promotions and premiums.
For details contact: Special Markets Department, Macmillan,
175 Fifth Ave., New York, NY 10010.

For more information, please visit www.kingfisherbooks.com

Printed in China
10 9 8 7 6 5 4 3 2
2TR/1116/WKT/UG/128MA

# CONTENTS

# Introduction
## U.S. Presidents

The president of the United States has the most powerful job in the country. As head of the federal government, he gets fancy titles like "chief executive" and "leader of the free world." The decisions the president makes affect how much spare change people have in their pockets and whether there is help for those who are sick or out of work. As commander in chief of the armed forces, he can even lead the military in war. Some of the presidents you'll see in this book are dressed in military uniforms . . . In fact, each illustration gives a clue to the president's story and what he achieved (yep, they've all been men so far!). So, can you figure out why these guys are shown the way they are?

For all their power, these politicians are not superhuman. Like all of us, they sometimes do stupid things, have crazy ideas, and generally fumble their way through. This is why the Founding Fathers created a system of checks and balances, with the president, Congress, and the judiciary limiting one another's powers. So what does it take to become president? Well, you can't be younger than 35 years old, you must be a natural-born citizen, and you need to have lived in the United States for at least 14 years. C'mon, let's meet the people who made it to the top . . .

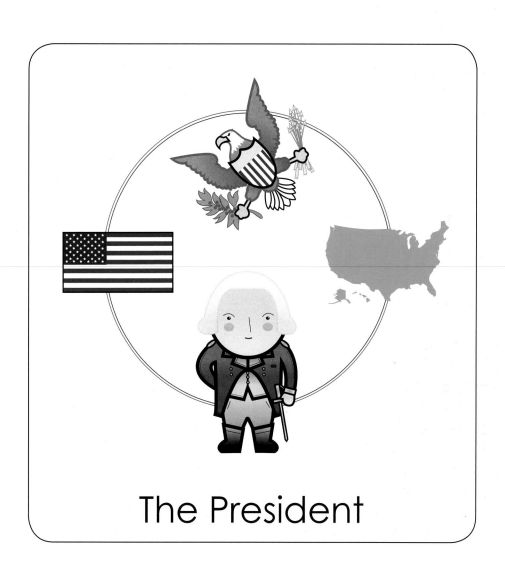

# The President

# The White House
Presidential Mansion

Gleaming white in the Washington, D.C. sunshine, the White House has been the home of American presidents since it was built in 1800. More than 40 chief executives and their families—plus an assortment of cows, goats, parrots, dogs, cats, horses, and even an alligator—have moved into 1600 Pennsylvania Avenue over the years.

The White House is not just the president's fancy crib (with its 132 rooms, 35 bathrooms, 8 staircases, and 3 elevators). It is also the center of the "executive branch" of the power triangle that makes up the U.S. government. The West Wing of this six-story joint is where it all happens, with the top dog working from the Oval Office. So, while the president *recommends* new laws, it is the "legislative" branch of government (Congress) that *makes* the laws and the "judicial" branch (the Supreme Court) that *reviews and interprets* the laws. That way, no single branch gets to take outright control. Although it was George Washington's idea to construct a federal capital on the Potomac River, he is the only president never to have slept in the presidential mansion.

The White House

# Chapter 1
## 18th- and 19th-Century Presidents

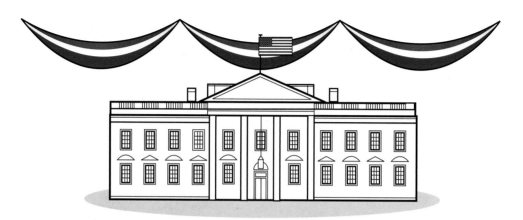

These presidential smarty-pants guided the country through its early years. The first four were all Founding Fathers—two of them even signed the Declaration of Independence. They were around for the American Revolution (1775–1783) and some of them drafted the Constitution. A bunch of (mostly) legal eagles and war heroes, these guys helped the infant country as it struggled to establish itself and define its borders. It's not easy starting a country and there was plenty of conflict, the biggest of which—the Civil War—threatened to tear the country apart. Read on to see what happened . . .

George
Washington

John
Adams

Thomas
Jefferson

James
Madison

James
Monroe

John Quincy
Adams

Andrew
Jackson

Martin
Van Buren

William Henry
Harrison

John
Tyler

James
K. Polk

Zachary
Taylor

Millard
Fillmore

Franklin
Pierce

James
Buchanan

Abraham
Lincoln

Andrew
Johnson

Ulysses S.
Grant

Rutherford
B. Hayes

James A.
Garfield

Chester A.
Arthur

Grover
Cleveland

Benjamin
Harrison

Grover
Cleveland

William
McKinley

# George Washington

■ 1st President    1789–1797

✳ One of the Founding Fathers of the United States
✳ A natural leader who defeated the British Empire
✳ His face appears on the $1 bill and the quarter

Tall, gracious, and ruggedly handsome, I was a Virginia gentleman and one revolutionary dude. As General Washington, I led the ragged troops of the Continental army in the American Revolution. We harassed the Brits for six years and, with the help of the French, sent 'em packing.

The nation's hero, I became chief executive after the war. I coined the term "Mr. President" and introduced the inaugural speech (proudly delivered wearing my new dentures made of gold, hippo ivory, and real teeth— cutting edge, or what!). Although the story about me and the cherry tree is a legend, there is a seed of truth in it: I was one honest guy. I never much liked politicians or politics, so before I retired to tend my farm at Mount Vernon, I warned Congress to avoid party politics. Fat chance!

● The first president of the United States
● The only president ever to be elected unanimously
● The only president whose horses had their teeth brushed every morning

# George Washington

"I hold the maxim no less applicable to public than to private affairs, that honesty is always the best policy."

11

# John Adams
## 2nd President   1797–1801

* Helped Jefferson draft the Declaration of Independence
* Wrote the Massachusetts state constitution
* Died on the same day as Jefferson (Fourth of July, 1826)

First Washington's vice president and then his successor, I always seemed to play second fiddle. Okay, I was no dashing, all-American hero, but I *was* a real-deal genius. As top dog I deserved great respect, but instead my critics called me "His Rotundity." Hilarious, I'm sure.

People loved it when I faced down the French, in a war that was never actually declared (they even called it the "Quasi-War"). But my real achievement was getting the infant United States out of training pants. The Founding Fathers were all for independence but couldn't agree on anything else. I was pals with Thomas Jefferson, but even we fought as president and vice president. My goal was a strong central government, but he wanted to stop Congress from meddling in people's affairs. Rifts were rife!

● The first president to live in the White House
● The only president from the Federalist Party
● The only president to have a vice president from the opposing party

# John Adams

"Fear is the foundation of most governments."

# Thomas Jefferson

## 3rd President    1801–1809

✳ This philosopher wrote the Declaration of Independence
✳ Founding Father who also founded the University of Virginia
✳ His face appears on the $2 bill and the nickel

They called me the "Sage of Monticello," and I was one wise sucker, I can assure you. I spoke five languages and liked to design things in my spare time—buildings, inventions, a clock for my house, even my own tombstone.

Before becoming president, I was Adams's veep (that's vice president to you), but I didn't see eye to eye with that Federalist nerd! I was pro liberty and against the call for a strong central government. I didn't do airs and graces—as president I sometimes met foreign dignitaries in my slippers and shirtsleeves! I purchased the Louisiana territory from Napoleon for $15 million, doubling the size of the United States, but not everything I did made sense. In the Declaration of Independence, I said all men are created equal, but like many other Virginia planters, I owned slaves.

● The first president to serve as secretary of state, vice president, and president
● The first president to be inaugurated at the Capitol in Washington, D.C.
● This president bathed his feet in ice-cold water every day

# Thomas Jefferson

"I have sworn upon the altar of God eternal hostility against every form of tyranny over the mind of man."

# James Madison

**4th President    1809–1817**

* Credited as the father of the Constitution
* At 5 ft., 4 in. (1.63 m), the shortest president ever
* Madison's face appeared on the $5,000 bill

Blessed with legal genius, not only did I help write the Constitution, but I also wrote the first ten amendments, now known as the Bill of Rights. I was all for "checks and balances," which made it tough for politicians to become corrupt while in power. Unfortunately, I was not as good at waging wars as I was at writing laws . . .

It was on my watch that the Brits burned down the White House during the War of 1812. They raided Washington, forced us to flee the presidential mansion, and had the nerve to eat our dinner before setting fire to the place. Luckily, my wife, Dolley, had the sense to pack a few things before she left, including a famous portrait of George Washington. The war ended with a truce and removed the threat of our becoming British subjects again. Phew!

● The first president to have been a member of the House of Representatives
● The last president to have been one of the 39 signers of the U.S. Constitution
● The only president to have two vice presidents die while he was in office

# James Madison

"As a man is said to have a right to his property,
he may be equally said to have a property in his rights."

# James Monroe
5th President    1817–1825

✴ Democratic-Republican and last Founding Father to hold office
✴ Won all but three of the 19 states when elected
✴ His Monroe Doctrine kept Europe's nose out of the Americas

Dapper, dashing, and spotlessly honest, I was the last president to have fought in the American Revolution. They called me the "Last Cocked Hat" because I pranced around in an outdated wig, hat, and breeches!

Voters shunned the Federalists for opposing the War of 1812, and the White House was mine for the taking! My presidency heralded the "Era of Good Feelings" because of the groovy vibes I brought to the country. People stuck with me through both an economic depression, in 1819, and the Missouri Compromise of 1820—that was a toughie! This bill made slavery in the West illegal north of the 36°30' line of latitude, except in Missouri. It allowed that state to join the Union as a slave state, despite entry having been denied in 1819.

● The first president to ride on a steamboat
● The last president to die on the Fourth of July
● The only president to have a foreign capital named after him (Monrovia, Liberia)

# James Monroe

"The best form of government is that which is most likely to prevent the greatest sum of evil."

# John Quincy Adams
## 6th President    1825–1829

✳ Was foreign minister to the Netherlands, Portugal, and Russia
✳ Penned a mighty 50-volume diary from 1779 to 1848
✳ The only ex-president to serve in the House of Representatives

Having a demanding father gives you a lot to live up to. But when your dad was the second president of the United States, you had better get with the program! I was up at 5:00 A.M. every day. I'd been the brains behind the Monroe Doctrine and, heck, I made the top job.

But it did not go well. One of four Democratic-Republicans to run for election, I came in second to Andrew Jackson. Henry Clay and I had to pool our votes to get the majority, and that upset the others big time! Diplomatic skills that had wowed Presidents Washington and Madison were no match for a Congress filled with backstabbers. Passing legislation was hard, to say the least, and my time in office was short-lived. I put the first pool table in the White House, but I was no lounge lizard—I left that to my pet alligator!

● The first president to be photographed (after presidency, in 1843)
● The last president to have switched from federalist sympathies to republican
● The only president to go skinny-dipping in the Potomac River every day

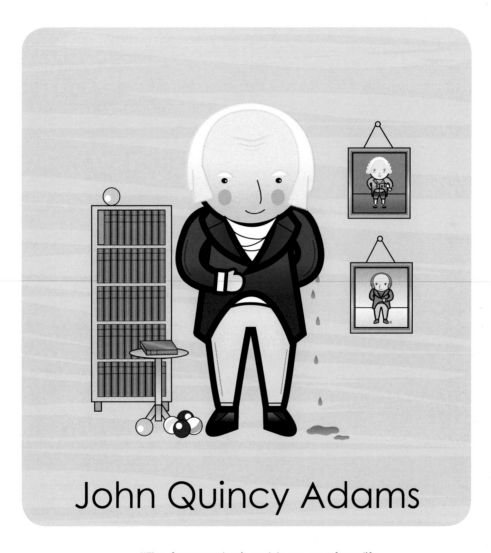

# John Quincy Adams

"The four most miserable years of my life
were my four years in the presidency."

# Andrew Jackson

## 7th President    1829–1837

✸ Skull-cracking hothead and hero of the War of 1812
✸ This Democrat eliminated the national debt in 1835
✸ "Old Hickory" is depicted on the $20 bill

I was a fighter! Tall, stick-thin, and hard as nails, I was born in a log cabin. I joined the Continental army at age 13 and lived through wars, illnesses, and duels . . . and bore the scars to boot. Cursed with an inflated sense of honor, I challenged all who crossed me to pistols at dawn!

As president I really took charge, vetoing bills passed by Congress and telling the states and the banks what to do. Most people loved me, while others mocked me with the moniker King Andrew. I sent soldiers to evict more than 15,000 Cherokee from the Southeast. Many of them died traveling on the "Trail of Tears" to reservations in Oklahoma. Later on, I survived an assassination attempt. Amazingly, both my assailant's pistols failed to fire. He got it in the neck when I thrashed him mercilessly with my cane!

● The first president to ride a steam-powered train
● The last president to have been a prisoner of war
● The only president to have a state capital named after him before taking office

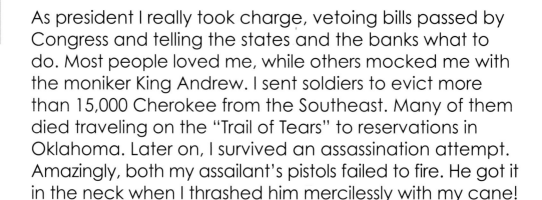

# Andrew Jackson

"The people are the government, administering it by their agents; they are the government, the sovereign power."

# Martin Van Buren
## 8th President    1837–1841

☀ One of the founders of the Democratic Party
☀ This one-term president was "Martin Van Ruin" to his enemies
☀ Had steam heating installed in the White House

A canny New Yorker and string puller extraordinaire, I could always be relied on to find a fix. But I came to power just as a bunch of bank failures created food shortages and sparked riots.

Born in a tavern, I proved that humble origins were no impediment to reaching for the top! A "little squirt"—just 5 ft., 6 in. (1.68m)—with muttonchop sideburns, I formed a solid partnership with Andrew Jackson. Veep during his second term, I continued his policy of "resettling" Native Americans. Some called me the "Little Magician" for my deft handling of party politics—boy, I knew how to play the game—but my magic failed me in the worst economic downturn that the United States would see until 1929. Once the panic had set in, I was on the road to ruin!

● The first president not born under British rule
● The last president to serve as secretary of state, vice president, and president
● The only president to speak English as a second language (his first was Dutch)

# Martin Van Buren

"The two happiest days of my life were those of my entrance upon the office and my surrender of it."

# William Henry Harrison

## 9th President    1841

✳ The first president from the Whig Party
✳ A battle-hardened, plainspoken gent with ten children
✳ Lost the race for the presidency to Van Buren in 1836

They called me "Granny." I may have been old, but I never forgot my promises . . . I said I wouldn't run for a second term and, by golly, I didn't! Thirty days is all you got from me—the shortest term of any president.

My heroics against the Native Americans at Tippecanoe River in 1811 left quite an impression, even 30 years later, so I was a shoo-in for office. I ran the best campaign ever—the first with cider, songs, and slogans, such as "Van is a used-up man" and "Tippecanoe and Tyler, too." These struck a chord with voters, and they booted Van Buren out. I wanted my inaugural address to be just as impressive and made it extra long and full of Latin. To show how tough I was, I delivered it in shirtsleeves in the bitter cold. Sadly, I caught pneumonia and died.

● The first president to die in office
● The last president to be born before the Declaration of Independence
● The only president to have studied to become a doctor

# William Henry Harrison

"A decent and manly examination of the acts of government should be not only tolerated, but encouraged."

# John Tyler
## 10th President   1841–1845

☀ Vice president at the time of Harrison's death
☀ Brought Florida into the Union and "annexed" Texas
☀ Had 15 children—more than any other U.S. president

When Harrison died unexpectedly, I came galloping from my Virginia plantation to take the reins (abandoning a game of marbles I'd been playing). There were no rules for this scenario, so I let it be known that I was the new president. Many called me "His Accidency," but there would be none of this "acting president" malarkey for me!

Like Harrison, I was a Whig, but I was also my own man. When I vetoed a Whig bill, all but one of my cabinet secretaries resigned and I was thrown out of my own party! Stubborn as a mule, I formed a new cabinet. While politicians fumed and chased their own tails, I expanded the national boundaries. At the close of my presidency, in cahoots with James K. Polk, I wangled a resolution to bring Texas into the Union, making war with Mexico a sure thing.

● The first president not to give an inaugural address
● The first president to marry while in office
● The only president to join the Confederacy (after presidency, in 1861)

# John Tyler

"I can never consent to being dictated to
as to what I shall or shall not do."

# James K. Polk
## 11th President  1845–1849

✹ At 49, this Democrat was the youngest president to date
✹ Known as "Young Hickory," thanks to Andrew Jackson's support
✹ Increased the size of the United States by 50 percent

Smartly dressed and slick-haired, I started out bright-eyed and bushy-tailed. My stirring speeches got me nicknamed "Napoleon of the Stump," but I was a man of action! If I said I'd do something, by golly, I'd get it done!

It was our "Manifest Destiny" to expand our territory from east coast to west, so I fixed on busting our boundaries (at some cost). I set the Texas border at the Rio Grande and fought Mexico for it, cunningly taking California and areas of the Southwest at the same time. I also signed a treaty with the Brits to bring Oregon into the Union. Some people called for slavery to be extended in the states we'd gotten in the war with Mexico. With my term in office over, it wasn't up to me. Having worked insanely hard, I left the office unpopular and dog-tired—and died soon after.

● The first president to be called a "dark horse" on account of being little known
● The first president to have his nomination widely reported by telegraph
● This president wrote a long (and boring) diary entry on handshaking

# James K. Polk

"No president who performs his duties faithfully and
conscientiously can have any leisure."

# Zachary Taylor
## 12th President 1849–1850

☀ A Whig president who'd been a tough military campaigner
☀ Known as "Old Rough and Ready," he wouldn't compromise
☀ Taylor was the second president to die in office

Shambling around in my old boots and shabby clothes, I was a funny-looking president. But that was me—plainspoken, straight-shootin', and homespun. I won my spurs in the West and on the battlefields of Mexico. I spat tobacco on the fancy White House carpets and kept my favorite horse, Old Whitey, on the lawn.

The Whigs brought me in to win their election, but I didn't see the point of toeing the party line—I just did what I was gonna do all along. Even though I owned slaves, I wouldn't expand slavery. This upset some Southern states, and they threatened to leave the Union. I promised to bring the army to any state that dared leave, while Congress tried to resolve things peacefully. I got sick while celebrating the Fourth of July and died as the debate dragged on.

● The first president not to have served previously in a public office
● The last president to own slaves while in office
● This president gave hair from his horse as a souvenir to guests

# Zachary Taylor

"I will not say I would not serve, if the good people
are imprudent enough to elect me."

# Millard Fillmore
## 13th President  1850–1853

✳ Stalwart and staid, this Whig tried to please everybody
✳ The second man to take office following a president's death
✳ Laid the groundwork for trade agreements with Japan

A simple frontier boy, I was born in a log cabin and educated in a one-room schoolhouse. I worked my way to the top, proving that a man could come from humble beginnings and rise to the highest office in the land. Unfortunately, "lackluster" seemed to be my middle name.

Unlike Old Rough and Ready, I was full to bursting with compromise. Trouble was brewing between slave-owning Southerners and industrial Northerners over the business of runaway slaves and import taxes. Plus there was a whole lot of fussing over territory and borders. It was, as I put it, "a season of embarrassment and alarm." Gee, I bent over backward to keep America's best interests at heart. But instead of pleasing folks, I made everyone unhappy. My party split for good and the Whigs were finished!

● The first president to have been born in the 1800s
● The first president to install a cooking stove at the White House
● The last president from the Whig party

# Millard Fillmore

"May God save the country,
for it is evident that the people will not."

# Franklin Pierce
### 14th President 1853–1857

☀ A "doughface"—a Northerner with Southern sympathies
☀ Delivered his inaugural speech from memory
☀ This Democrat steered the country toward civil war

Dark and dashing, I made the ladies quiver and sigh.
Had there been a vote for America's cutest president,
I'd have won hands down! Sadly, my time at the top
coincided with personal tragedy. My son was killed in
a train crash and I struggled to cope at the White House.

Despite feckless Fillmore's compromises, the nation seemed
intent on civil war. Sick as a dog, I was helpless to stop it.
I decided to let settlers in Kansas territory make up their
own minds on whether to be a slave state (which ignored
Monroe's Missouri Compromise). Boy, was that a bad idea!
Before you could say "emancipation," people were busy
killing each other. The situation was almost just as bad in
Congress—some senators armed themselves after a fight
broke out! This was just a sign of the unrest yet to come.

● The first president to employ a full-time bodyguard
● The last president to have been injured in the Mexican-American War
● The only president to have been a native of New Hampshire

# Franklin Pierce

"I have never believed that actual disruption
of the Union can occur without blood."

# James Buchanan
## 15th President 1857–1861

✳ This doughface Democrat was widely seen as a failure
✳ "Old Buck" didn't prepare for war or try to prevent it
✳ Pledged not to seek a second term in office from the start

I'd been in politics more than 40 years by the time the country pinned its hopes on me to mend its breaking heart. But instead of finding ways to fix our divided nation, I managed to frustrate everyone. Civil war was a-knockin' at the door, and I opened up and let it come right on in.

Northern states thought slavery was wrong and should be abolished, while Southern states depended on it and wanted it extended. What was I to do? My indecision split the Democrats and guaranteed victory at the next election for the Republicans (a newly formed party of Whigs and Democrats with Northern sympathies). Well, as soon as Abe Lincoln won, slave states started deserting the Union like rats from a sinking ship. Me? Oh, I just did nothing while I waited to leave office.

● The first president to have states secede from the Union
● The last president to have been secretary of state (in 1845, prior to presidency)
● The only president to remain a bachelor (unmarried) his whole life

# James Buchanan

"Liberty must be allowed to work out its natural results;
and these will, ere long, astonish the world."

# Abraham Lincoln
## 16th President 1861–1865

✷ Kept the United States as one nation with liberty for all
✷ "Honest Abe" was assassinated by John Wilkes Booth in 1865
✷ This Republican appears on the $5 bill and the penny

Toweringly tall, all chinstrap beard and flappy ears, I was known for my trademark stovepipe hat. Born and raised in a log cabin, I'd had a pretty lean education, but I worked hard to become a lawyer.

They call me the "Great Emancipator" because I abolished slavery in the United States. The way I saw it, keeping slaves made a mockery of our country's goal of liberty for all. Sadly, 11 Southern states saw things differently. In 1861, they formed the breakaway Confederate States of America. I made it clear to those rebels that it was not *their* duty to break the Union apart but *mine* to uphold it and, come what may, I would defend it! Tough words, I know, but I meant every last one. My determination led to civil war and victory for the Union.

● The first president to appear on a minted coin
● The only president to hold a patent (for a boat buoyancy device)
● This president was known for keeping papers (quite literally) under his hat

# Abraham Lincoln

"With malice toward none; with charity for all . . .
let us strive on to finish the work we are in."

# Andrew Johnson

✳ Gritty Democrat and first president of the Reconstruction Era
✳ One of the few presidents without a formal education
✳ The only Southern senator not to resign during the Civil War

Leather-faced and crotchety, I'm the "Tailor of Tennessee." As a senator from Tennessee I stayed put in the Senate when my state pulled out of the Union in 1861. This made me so unpopular in my home state that I had to give speeches with a loaded revolver on the lectern!

I buddied up with Lincoln as his second-term veep. Abe thought rubbing shoulders with a Southern Democrat would help restore peace after the Civil War. With him gone, I left rebuilding the South in the hands of state governments— the people who'd supported slavery and fought the Union! Their new laws were unfair toward African Americans. Radical Republicans in Congress took control, and when I got in their way, they impeached me. I was acquitted by the Senate but could flex my muscles no more.

● The first president not to have had a legal or military career
● The last president to teach himself to read
● The only president to be elected to the United States Senate after he left office

# Andrew Johnson

"Our government springs from, and was made for,
the people—not the people for the government."

# Ulysses S. Grant
## 18th President 1869–1877

✸ No-nonsense Republican president
✸ Blockbuster Union general during the Civil War
✸ His presidency saw African Americans given the right to vote

My childhood nickname was "Useless," but I was born to serve my country. Rugged and outdoorsy, I joined the Union army, rising to general in chief. While I engineered brilliant victories, my battles were infamous for their gore (although I couldn't stand the sight of blood myself).

I was determined to advance civil rights for African Americans. So I pushed through the 15th Amendment, giving freedmen the vote, and came down really hard on white supremacists. But while I'd been a sparkling general, I was a truly stinking president. I allowed cabinet secretaries to run their departments as they liked and protected my men when it would have been better to weed out the bad eggs. Sure enough, I was soon surrounded by schemers, scoundrels, and scandals.

● The first president to change his name legally (from Hiram Ulysses Grant)
● The last president of the 19th century to serve two consecutive terms
● This president was given a speeding ticket while serving in office (riding his horse!)

# Ulysses S. Grant

"Laws are to govern all alike—
those opposed as well as those who favor them."

# Rutherford B. Hayes
## 19th President  1877–1881

✳ A criminal lawyer and fair-minded Republican
✳ His controversial election was decided by a commission
✳ Held the first Easter-egg roll on the White House lawn

With the bad taste left by Grant, I was just what the Republicans needed—a straitlaced, middle-of-the-road kinda guy. Careful, meticulous, and full of good intentions, I was also full of holes from fighting in the Civil War.

My election was one of the closest in U.S. history—I won by a single electoral vote and was dubbed "Rutherfraud" by my opponents. Saintly as ever, I pledged to serve only one term, during which I fought to preserve the Force Acts that made it illegal to stop someone from voting because of the color of their skin. But I also returned home rule to the Southern states and left African Americans to fend for themselves. At home, I was a model of decorum. My wife, "Lemonade Lucy," banned alcohol in the White House, and we sang hymns every day.

● The first president to install a telephone in the White House
● The first president to visit the West Coast while in office
● The last president of the Reconstruction Era

# Rutherford B. Hayes

"I am a radical in thought (and principle)
and a conservative in method (and conduct)."

# James A. Garfield

■ 20th President   1881

❋ Full-bearded, ill-fated Republican president
❋ The second U.S. president to be assassinated
❋ Could write Latin and Greek simultaneously (using both hands)

I was the last of the log-cabin presidents, and my working life began as a canalside mule driver. After falling in the water 14 times and catching a fever, my old ma packed me off to school. I never looked back!

I had promise, I can tell you! I was pro civil rights; I saw the benefits of educating the electorate; and I had plans to reform the civil service. Who knows what I might have achieved? Not me, as I was shot after just four months in office! You see, as president it was not unusual to receive requests from the public. So when one Charles Guiteau wanted to be consul general in Paris, I thought nothing of it. Sadly, he thought of nothing else and came after me with a gun when I turned him down. Doctors tried everything, but after 11 weeks, I met my maker.

● The first left-handed president
● The last president not to have vetoed (rejected) any bills
● This president came up with a proof of the Pythagorean theorem

# James A. Garfield

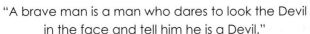

"A brave man is a man who dares to look the Devil
in the face and tell him he is a Devil."

# Chester A. Arthur
## 21st President   1881–1885

☀ "Prince Arthur" was a dandy Republican schmoozer
☀ The fourth veep to succeed a dead president
☀ Had a deadly kidney disease he kept secret from everyone

A golden boy (almost) of America's Gilded Age, I had elegance, taste, and style. I broke a tradition going back three presidents by being smooth-faced, except for the full-blown mustache, and had 80 pairs of pants. I took the reins after Garfield's death—another veep stepping into the breach . . . or should that be breeches? (Ha, ha!)

You could call me the butterfly president. Why? Well, I started out as a grub. I was mixed up with a bunch of maggotlike crooks at the New York Custom House and was well known for "dishing out the pork"—giving political favors for money. But I surprised everybody after I became president, pushing through a reform of the civil service that tackled bribes, among other things. I went from being distrusted to being widely admired by all.

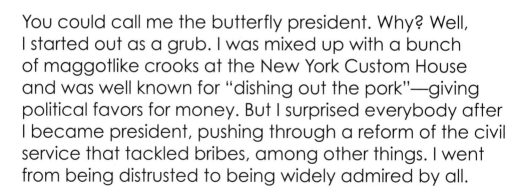

● The first president to travel to Wyoming (in 1883)
● The last president to sport whiskers in the shape of muttonchops
● The only president to have been a school principal

# Chester A. Arthur

"Men may die, but the fabric of our free institutions remains unshaken."

# Grover Cleveland
## ■ 22nd and 24th President 1885–1889; 1893–1897

❋ This Democrat had two separate turns at the presidency
❋ "Uncle Jumbo" is known as the most honest president ever
❋ Got married at the White House while in office

I was a man of great conviction—a bit punchy and a bit paunchy, but I always told the truth. My reputation for honesty and reform gave me a boost when I ran for president. I managed to sway a bunch of disillusioned Republicans ("Mugwumps") to vote for me and became the first Democrat to be elected since the Civil War.

I believed in equal opportunities for all. I worked like a brute to check every bill that crossed my desk, and in my first term, I vetoed twice as many bills as all the previous U.S. presidents put together! Narrowly beaten by Benjamin Harrison in the 1888 race, I was back and punching hard in 1893, only to flounder in the face of economic depression. I was finished! It would be another 16 years before a Democrat took office again.

● The first president whose Christmas tree had electric lights
● The only president to have had a baby born in the White House
● The only president to have two nonconsecutive terms in office

# Grover Cleveland

"What is the use of being elected or reelected unless you stand for something?"

# Benjamin Harrison

## 23rd President 1889–1893

✺ Stodgy Republican who failed to make a big impression
✺ Shortness of stature made "Little Ben" a figure of fun for some
✺ Was preceded and succeeded by the same president

Some people called me the "Human Iceberg," but don't go thinking that means I was a cool guy. Quite the opposite, in fact. While I was a very good public speaker, one-on-one I was as chilly as a polar bear.

So why me? Well, aside from being Old Tippecanoe Harrison's grandson, I was the party favorite. With the help of a crack team of electioneering hotshots (and a hefty campaign fund), I beat Grover Cleveland. I mustered 100,000 fewer popular votes than His Obstinacy but carried the Electoral College 233 to 168. (Pardon me for the political jargon—it means more people actually voted for him but more state electoral votes went to me. Got it?) I failed to connect with the nation and, although I might not have done anything very wrong, history has forgotten me.

● The first president to have electric lights installed at the White House
● The last president to have a beard
● The only president whose grandfather was a former president (W. H. Harrison)

# Benjamin Harrison

"We Americans have no commission from
God to police the world."

# William McKinley

## ■ 25th President  1897–1901

✷ A Republican who ran a front-porch campaign
✷ Brought boom times and further expanded U.S. territory
✷ Was assassinated by the anarchist Leon Czolgosz, in 1901

A real, bona fide nice guy, though I also had a cunning streak running deep beneath the surface. I was one polished operator, I can tell you—the sort of person who made people think that my ideas were theirs. *Wink, wink!*

I was a real friend to the press, sharing news of what went on in the corridors of power (well, the stuff I wanted them to know about!). I had a craving for foreign territory and stood to gain from helping liberate Cuba from Spain. The battleship *Maine* blew sky-high in Havana harbor, killing 266 U.S. sailors, so I took Spain to war. In just 100 days, Cuba was free. The U.S. got Puerto Rico, the Philippines, and Guam in the process—*gracias, amigos!* What with Hawaii annexed and the economy booming, things were looking good. Sadly for me, Czolgosz saw things differently.

● The first president to hold regular press briefings
● The last president to have served in the Civil War
● This president had a pair of Angora kittens as pets

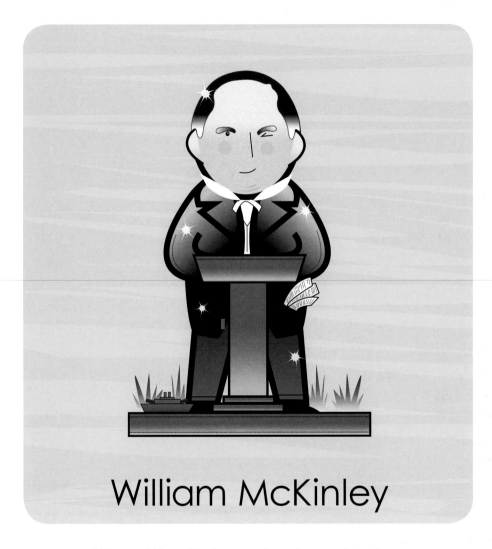

# William McKinley

"We need Hawaii just as much and a good deal more
than we did California; it is Manifest Destiny."

# Chapter 2
## 20th- and 21st-Century Presidents

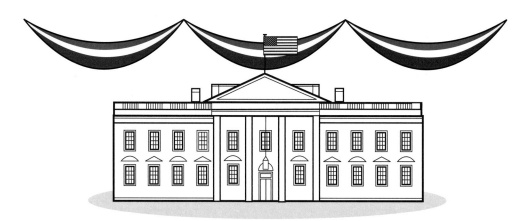

Welcome to the gang of rogues, rascals, and reformers who saw the United States right through the 20th century and well into the 21st. And what exciting times these were, with technology moving apace and the population expanding like never before. The challenges came thick and fast, yet these guys turned the country into a global superpower, saving it once or twice from the brink of ruin. There was a fair amount of bloodshed, too, with two world wars; a war in Korea and another in Vietnam; two wars in Iraq; and a war on terror. And let's not forget the long-lasting and frosty Cold War . . .

Theodore
Roosevelt

William
Howard Taft

Woodrow
Wilson

Warren G.
Harding

Calvin
Coolidge

Herbert
Hoover

Franklin D.
Roosevelt

Harry S.
Truman

Dwight D.
Eisenhower

John F.
Kennedy

Lyndon B.
Johnson

Richard
Nixon

Gerald
Ford

Jimmy
Carter

Ronald
Reagan

George
H. W. Bush

Bill
Clinton

George
W. Bush

Barack
Obama

Donald J.
Trump

# Theodore Roosevelt
## 26th President   1901–1909

✷ Robust Republican and inspiration behind the teddy bear
✷ A model president and the first of the 20th century
✷ This hunting fanatic once bagged 17 lions on safari

Ten-hut! With oodles of energy, I was always ready for a little rough-and-tumble. I rode with the Rough Riders in the Spanish-American War and lost the sight in one eye from boxing with a military aide at the White House.

I bounced onto the scene at age 42—the youngest president ever. With me at the helm, the chief exec's role just got bigger and bigger. Boy, did I whip the country into shape! I started with "trust-busting"—dismantling massive corporations. I made laws to protect workers but, at the same time, broke up strikes. I wanted to make sure that the system worked in everyone's best interests. But you couldn't say I was coldhearted. Out hunting one day, I refused to kill a bear cub. "Teddy's bear" inspired the smash-hit stuffed toy and bedtime favorite.

● The first president to go under the sea in a submarine
● The last president to be carved into Mount Rushmore, pince-nez and all
● This president and his family could all walk on stilts

# Theodore Roosevelt

"Speak softly and carry a big stick; you will go far."

# William Howard Taft

■ 27th President   1909–1913

❋ Yale heavyweight-wrestling champion, AKA "Big Bill"
❋ Went on to become chief justice of the United States
❋ Got just 23 percent of the vote running for a second term

Voted in after Mr. Charisma, I failed to match Teddy's raw vitality and aptitude for playing the political game. A legal eagle at heart, I felt more comfortable in the Supreme Court than at the White House (in more ways than one after getting wedged in the bathtub!).

Roosevelt wanted me to fill his shoes, and who was I to argue with that? I kept big corporations under control, but fellow Republicans thought my leadership skills stank. The party split and even Teddy turned against me. A second term was out of the question. I loved baseball and, in 1910, I was the first president to throw a ceremonial pitch to start the season. I liked my milk fresh in the morning and kept a cow on the White House lawn. Unlike me, that bovine beauty always delivered.

● The first president to have a presidential car
● The last president to wear a mustache
● The only president to come in third in a presidential election (in 1912)

# William Howard Taft

"Presidents come and go, but the Supreme Court goes on forever."

# Woodrow Wilson
## 28th President   1913–1921

✴ Hectoring Democrat who promised a "New Freedom"
✴ An academic and former president of Princeton University
✴ Known as Woodrow, although his first name was Thomas

Pinch-nosed and strict, I was the "Schoolmaster"—the only president with a PhD. You may think I was a bit of a stiff, but you'd be wrong there. Beneath my flinty exterior lay a passionate, buccaneering spirit.

I was committed to fairness for all. That's why I pushed for progressive legislation on trade and banking. In 1920, women won the right to vote. I tried to keep America out of World War I, but when German submarines started sinking U.S. ships bound for England, I tore off my scholar's robes and let rip. The Germans even tried to get Mexico to attack the United States, but Mexico chose not to. After Germany surrendered, I fought hard for a long-lasting peace and was awarded a Nobel Peace Prize and (sadly) a paralyzing stroke for my efforts.

● The first president to meet the pope while in office
● The last president to marry during his time in office
● The only president buried in Washington, D.C.

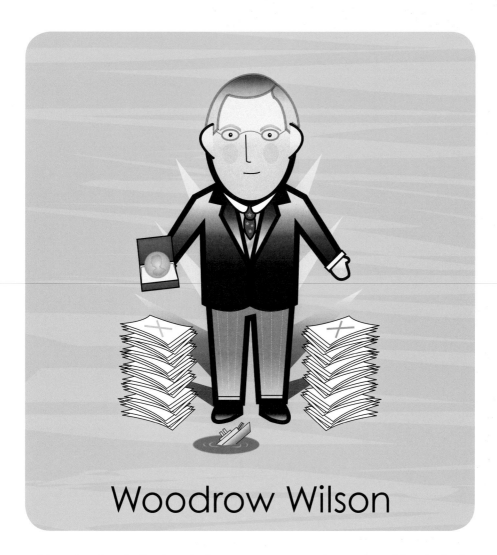

# Woodrow Wilson

"America lives in the heart of every man everywhere who wishes to find a region where he will be free to work out his destiny as he chooses."

# Warren G. Harding

**29th President   1921–1923**

✳ "Wobbly Warren" was a leisure-seeking Republican
✳ A do-nothing president who put his low friends in high places
✳ Died of a heart attack before scandal overtook him

Today, I'm dubbed the worst U.S. president ever, but you couldn't have met a nicer guy. They call me a card-playing slob—okay, so I liked to cut the deck! They say I was handpicked by a bunch of high-level fixers in a smoke-filled room. So? I got the presidency, didn't I?

My wife, the "Duchess," loved it. But while I may have looked the part, I didn't much like the job. If you ask me, I felt more at home playing poker and golf. On the plus side, I got to meet lots of important guys. Not bad for a newspaperman from Ohio! Although my style was "hands-off," some shadier dudes in my cabinet were very much "hands-on." One got caught taking bribes for the oil rights in Teapot Dome and Elk Hills. Too bad, because today it's just about all I'm remembered for.

● The first president to receive more than 10 million votes (16,152,200)
● The last president to chew tobacco while in office
● This president bet the White House china on a game of cards . . . and lost!

# Warren G. Harding

"Forget that I'm president of the United States. I'm Warren Harding, playing poker with friends, and I'm going to beat [the heck] out of them!"

# Calvin Coolidge
## 30th President   1923–1929

✳ This staid Republican took charge when Harding died
✳ The only U.S. president to be born on Independence Day
✳ No other president worked harder to do so little

Cool as a tall glass of lemonade on a hot day, I was a pretty laid-back kinda guy! After Wobbly Warren, it was my job to make the presidency something to be proud of once again. My achievements may be few, but at least I can claim to have done that!

Upright, upstanding, and moral in outlook, that was me, all right. I was a man of few words—the less said, the better was my motto. In fact, *doing* less was good, too. These were the Roaring Twenties, a time of "Coolidge Prosperity." Everybody was busy getting rich, and it was better all around if I left 'em to it. In fact, I was so hands-off that at times it looked like I wasn't even holding on! The only reins I really took hold of were those on my electric exercise horse. Gee, the fun I had!

● The last president to own a pet raccoon
● The only president sworn in late at night, by kerosene lamp . . . by his dad!
● This president was photographed wearing a Native American headdress

# Calvin Coolidge

"I favor the policy of economy, not because I wish to save money, but because I wish to save people."

# Herbert Hoover

## 31st President   1929–1933

* This Republican was known as the "Great Engineer"
* Ex-mining engineer who contributed to at least 40 books
* Boulder Dam was renamed Hoover Dam in his honor

My presidency coincided with hard times. Known for my problem-solving skills, I thought I could turn the nation's fortunes around. But, no matter what I tried, the country remained depressed. The strain of it turned my hair white!

We'd ripped through the twenties with unprecedented prosperity. Poverty seemed a thing of the past. But then Black Tuesday followed Black Thursday and that was it—the stock crash of 1929 and the start of the Great Depression. I knew I had to keep people working, and I funded many public projects, but I refused to open the country's coffers directly to the unemployed. "Hooverville" slums grew all around, and folks began to say I was uncaring and cruel. (Eating seven-course dinners when many were on handouts didn't help.) Most people weren't sad to see me go.

● The first president to give his salary away (JFK did, too)
● The last Republican president for 20 years
● The only president who was fluent in Mandarin Chinese

# Herbert Hoover

"We must not be misled by the claim that the source of all wisdom is in the government."

# Franklin D. Roosevelt

■ 32nd President 1933–1945

✳ This legendary Democrat served 12 years in office
✳ His "New Deal" helped America fight the Great Depression
✳ His face is on the dime

Not two, not three, but *four* election victories, that's FDR! I was a boundless ball of enthusiasm and energy, and almost nobody knew that my legs had been paralyzed by polio when I was 39. Yep! That was my business!

America was on its knees in 1933, with 13 million people out of a job. My country needed me, and I got to work. My strategy? Do something—and if that doesn't work, do something else! I started spending big-time. I taxed the rich and began a massive work-relief program for the unemployed. Meantime, my reassuring radio "fireside chats" soothed the nation. When Japan bombed the U.S. Navy in Pearl Harbor in 1941, I led the country into World War II. Sadly, I died of a brain hemorrhage shortly after starting my fourth term.

● The first president to appear on television
● The last president to be inaugurated on March 4 (after which it was January 20)
● The only president to win four successive election victories

# Franklin D. Roosevelt

"The only thing we have to fear is fear itself."

# Harry S. Truman
## 33rd President 1945–1953

* Nearsighted Democrat with farsighted vision
* Led with his "Fair Deal" when FDR died unexpectedly
* The "S" in his name does not stand for anything

I had FDR's size 12s to fill, and no one believed I could do it. We'd all but defeated the Germans by then, but World War II was still raging in the Pacific. The way I saw it (and told anyone within earshot), the buck stopped with me!

I had some pretty tough decisions to make. I gave the order to drop atomic bombs on Japan, which caused thousands of deaths. This brutal action resulted in Japan's surrender and an end to the war. After that, I just kept going! I put a stop to racial segregation in the military; I joined NATO; I delivered aid to Europe with the Marshall Plan; and I airlifted provisions to West Berlin when the Soviets cut it off. I was determined to stop Communism from spreading (a policy later called the Truman Doctrine). Who knew it would lead the country into the Korean War?

● The first president to have his inauguration broadcast on television (in 1949)
● The first president to have taken office during wartime
● The only 20th-century president without a college degree

# Harry S. Truman

"No nation on this globe should be more internationally minded than America because it was built by all nations."

# Dwight D. Eisenhower
■ 34th President   1953–1961

✳ A Republican and a really trusty guy who kept the peace
✳ This cold warrior had a "New Look" nuclear strategy
✳ "Ike" loved golf and had a putting green at the White House

A regular Boy Scout, I was a five-star general who led his troops to victory in World War II. My presidential campaign slogan was "I like Ike" and, you know, people did just that!

I put interstate highways on the map. The idea was to help the military get around the country quickly should we face invasion (hey, these were scary times). Although I was a thoroughbred man o' war, I pledged myself to world peace. As good as my word, I ended the war in Korea. The military was itching to spend every last dime on rockets and bombs, but I favored the threat of a cheaper (nuclear) alternative to keep potential enemies at bay. Despite my best efforts, the Cold War with the Soviet Union got chillier. The launch of their satellite *Sputnik I* terrified us. We thought it might lead to a lethal weapon in orbit!

● The first president to use a helicopter to get around (*Marine One*)
● The only president to have served in both World War I and World War II
● This president had his paintings displayed in an art exhibition

# Dwight D. Eisenhower

"We must be ready to dare all for our country. For history does not long entrust the care of freedom to the weak or the timid."

# John F. Kennedy
## ■ 35th President   1961–1963

✳ The youngest man ever to win a presidential election (age 43)
✳ Established the Peace Corps volunteer program in 1961
✳ Assassinated in 1963 in Dallas, Texas, by Lee Harvey Oswald

Youthful, charming, and a World War II hero, I became a 20th-century icon. I inspired a whole generation of young Americans, while my wife, Jackie, wowed the nation with her pretty pearls and pillbox hats.

I was bursting with political potential, but my time in office brought mixed fortunes. I got my fingers burned giving the thumbs-up to an invasion of Cuba. The Communist Soviet Union shipped nuclear missiles to the island in response, and it took nimble diplomatic footwork to avoid all-out nuclear war. Things looked no better in South Vietnam when I okayed a plot to overthrow its president. At home, though, I promoted the space race and supported the civil rights movement. Who knows what I might have achieved had I not been shot dead after barely 1,000 days in office?

● The first president to have been born in the 20th century
● The last president to wear a stovepipe hat to his inauguration
● The only president to have been a Roman Catholic

# John F. Kennedy

"And so, my fellow Americans: ask not what your country can do for you—ask what you can do for your country."

# Lyndon B. Johnson
## 36th President   1963–1969

✳ This Democrat had a vision of a "Great Society"
✳ Appointed the first African-American Supreme Court justice
✳ His presidency saw U.S. astronauts orbit the Moon

I was no saint, that's for sure! I was a hard-talkin' Texan with a go-get-'em approach. Anyone'll tell you there was something about me that got right under the skin.

But, boy, did I deliver! Working 18-hour days, I nursed a nation reeling from the shock of JFK's death. I was determined to do the right thing, so I worked with Congress to introduce sweeping legislation. I waged the first war on poverty, passed the Civil Rights and Voting Rights acts, and brought in health care programs for the poor and elderly. I wowed the nation . . . until I committed the country more deeply to a jungle conflict in Vietnam. Who could have known that the war would cost 58,000 American lives? America lost faith in me and I bowed out as gracefully as I could.

● The last president to have a space center named after him
● The only president to be sworn in aboard *Air Force One*
● This president once worked as an elevator operator

# Lyndon B. Johnson

"All Americans must have the privileges of citizenship regardless of race. And they are going to have those privileges of citizenship regardless of race."

# Richard Nixon
## 37th President 1969–1974

☀ This paranoid Republican was obsessed with secrecy
☀ Pulled U.S. troops out of Vietnam, but fighting there continued
☀ "Tricky Dick" resigned to avoid impeachment over Watergate

People remember me as a shifty operator who liked to sail close to the wind. I loved to bowl, but it wasn't long before the lucky strikes stopped coming my way.

I'd always been a get-ahead kinda guy and my ambition took me all the way to the top. I did some good things: *Apollo 11* landed on the Moon, for starters. I managed to smooth relations with Communist China and the Soviets, and I signed a treaty limiting nuclear arms. America's silent majority liked me, but I was still jumpy; finally my paranoia got the better of me. When my guys raided the opposition's offices, they were caught red-handed, and my attempts to cover it up exploded into the Watergate scandal. Like Humpty Dumpty, when I fell, no one could put me back together again.

● The first president to visit Communist China
● The first presidential candidate to campaign in all 50 states
● The only president to resign from office

# Richard Nixon

"When the president does it, that means that it is not illegal."

# Gerald Ford
## ■ 38th President  1974–1977

❋ This affable Republican had a reputation for clumsiness
❋ An Eagle Scout who loved football, boxing, skiing, and golf
❋ The longest-lived president, dying at 93 years and 165 days

Laid-back and friendly, I was the dreamy antidote to the Nixon nightmare. I was a happy-go-lucky hunk with an easy grin. I could have played pro football with the Green Bay Packers or Detroit Lions, but I chose law instead.

Nixon's veep during the unfolding of the Watergate scandal (my predecessor, Spiro T. Agnew, having resigned over tax evasion), I stepped up when Tricky Dick resigned. People seemed to like me and things went really well . . . for about a month. Then I nixed it by granting Nixon a full pardon. I know! But I thought it would clear the air of Watergate and let me get on with my Whip Inflation Now campaign (no easy task with a largely Democratic Congress). I was out of luck—the public lost faith in me, and I never won a second term.

● The only president to serve as both veep and chief exec without being elected
● The only president to survive assassination attempts by not one, but two, women
● The only president to have died in one year and been buried in the next

# Gerald Ford

"I assume the presidency under extraordinary circumstances . . . This is an hour of history that troubles our minds and hurts our hearts."

# Jimmy Carter
## 39th President   1977–1981

☀ "Jimmy Who?" was a Democrat and an outsider
☀ Presided over an energy crisis that he just couldn't fix
☀ The first president from the Deep South since the Civil War

I was the God-fearing peanut farmer with the cut-and-paste smile. America celebrated its 200th birthday in the year I was elected and got a folksy kinda guy as chief. Peanut anyone?

Things were a mess, and the country needed my down-home principles. The oil crisis of 1973 had left its mark. Fuel was pricey and in short supply. Lines at gas stations got long and angry. I looked for ways of conserving energy and reducing our reliance on foreign oil, but things were tough! I got sparring Egypt and Israel to make peace, but when I bungled the rescue of U.S. hostages in Iran, people decided they'd had enough of me. I've devoted the rest of my life to working for peace and healing rifts, and was awarded the Nobel Peace Prize in 2002.

● The first president to have been born in a hospital
● The last president not to preside over a war
● The only president to report seeing a UFO

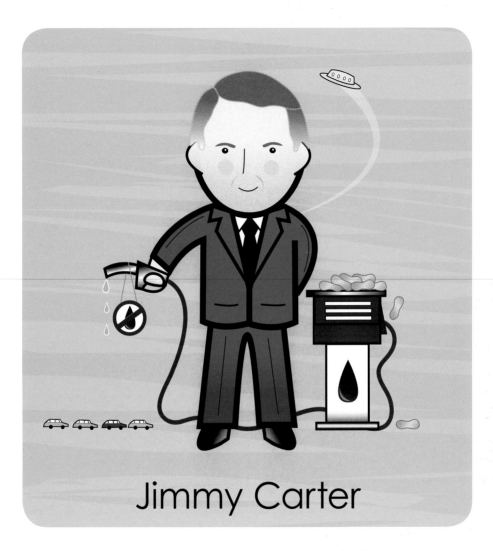

# Jimmy Carter

"America did not invent human rights. In a very real sense,
it is the other way round. Human rights invented America."

# Ronald Reagan
■ 40th President   1981–1989

☀ The wisecracking Republican with an acting career
☀ This "Great Communicator" helped end the Cold War
☀ His economic policies were nicknamed "Reaganomics"

I was the guy who duked it out with Russia, the "evil empire," and won. Ever optimistic, I aimed to put defense systems in space and a roar back into the United States.

Getting shot just weeks into my presidency earned me the sympathy of the nation. I set about passing legislation to boost the economy—and not without success. But I also increased spending on defense, which landed the country deeper in debt. Then I allowed the illegal funding of rebels in Nicaragua using money from arms sales to Iran! Well, they didn't call me the "Teflon president" for nothing—dirt just didn't stick to me. I was one popular guy! I worked closely with the Soviet premier Mikhail Gorbachev to trash hundreds of nuclear missiles and take the sting out of the Cold War.

● The last president to win almost 100 percent of the electoral vote (in 1984)
● The only president to have been a movie star
● This president was also president of the Screen Actors Guild

# Ronald Reagan

"It is time for us to realize that we're too great
a nation to limit ourselves to small dreams."

# George H. W. Bush
■ 41st President  1989–1993

☀ A Republican Texas oilman with Northern origins
☀ Led an international coalition, in 1991, during the Gulf War
☀ A diplomat who kept on good terms with Russia and China

My star qualities were decency and fairness. As well as having an impressive political résumé, I was a wealthy man, an oil industry tycoon. I gave the office all I had but, for some, it just wasn't enough.

The world was changing shape, with the Soviet Union crumbling, and I was pretty glad not to intervene. Meanwhile, the United States had its first run-in with the Iraqi dictator, Saddam Hussein, who'd invaded his Persian Gulf neighbor Kuwait, in 1990. Before sending in our forces, I was careful to build an international posse. We liberated Kuwait and sent Saddam's men packing, little knowing that we'd face them again in years to come. Back home, the respect I'd won over Iraq was lost by tax hikes that I'd promised to avoid. I didn't win a second term.

● The first president to visit Singapore
● The last president to have fought in World War II—he flew 58 combat missions
● This president threw up while dining with the prime minister of Japan

# George H. W. Bush

"Read my lips: no new taxes."

# Bill Clinton
## 42nd President 1993–2001

* The first Democrat to serve two full terms since FDR
* A people person who played peacemaker on the world stage
* The second U.S. president to be impeached

Smooth-jawed and as sultry as my sax playing, I was a wily fox with an instinct for playing a situation. A political dynamo, I brought a new vision to the United States.

My running mate, Al Gore, and I took a hotshot team to the White House. Fueled on adrenaline and pulling crazy all nighters, we brought the good times back to America. The economy boomed, and reforms reflected our caring attitude toward those in greater need. My wife, Hillary, and I made a powerhouse duo. She even got an office in the West Wing! I did so much for the country but ruined my image with my . . . ahem . . . way with the ladies. Seedy scandals surfaced and I was accused of lying about one of them under oath. I was impeached and, although I was acquitted, my reputation paid a price.

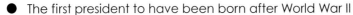

● The first president to have been born after World War II
● The last president to have shaken JFK's hand
● The only president whose wife became a U.S. senator and secretary of state

# Bill Clinton

"When we make college more affordable,
we make the American dream more achievable."

# George W. Bush
■ 43rd President  2001–2009

☀ An easy-going and likable Republican
☀ "Dubya" set up the Department of Homeland Security
☀ Declared war on terror and invaded Afghanistan and Iraq

I won the election against Al Gore by a whisker—it took more than a month to declare a winner. People laughed at my unique turn of phrase, but I said: just "don't misunderestimate me!"

The events of 9/11—the worst ever terrorist attacks on the United States—defined my presidency. I led a War on Terror overseas, chasing al-Qaeda culprits in Afghanistan, and at home, signing the Patriot Act, which allowed law enforcement officers to track, interrogate, and detain any citizen suspected of terrorism. Like my father before me, I set my sights on Saddam Hussein and invaded Iraq. As Commander-in-Chief, I saw it as a case of "good" versus "evil." I delivered tax cuts and sent aid following Hurricane Katrina in 2005, but some said it wasn't enough.

● The first president to be granted a state visit to the United Kingdom
● The last president whose father had also been president
● The only president to own a baseball team: part owner of the Texas Rangers

# George W. Bush

"Every nation in every region now has a decision to make:
Either you are with us or you are with the terrorists."

# Barack Obama

## ■ 44th President  2009–2017

✳ This Democrat was the first African-American president
✳ Won the Nobel Peace Prize in 2009
✳ Presided over a draw-down in Iraq, but violence continues

I am the man with the yes-we-can attitude. I symbolized hope for change. I am a supreme orator and my soaring speeches have melted the hearts of many.

Chaos is a polite term for what I faced when I took the reins: At home I battled with the fallout of global recession; abroad, the Middle East was on the brink of radical change. But I did not falter. My domestic policies saw 20 million Americans insured under Obamacare. I got the U.S. economy back on track and cut unemployment in half from its peak during the recession.  And when the militant group, the Islamic State, threatened to unsettle the Arab world, I focused my foreign policy on their terrorist activities. My big regret? I couldn't push through legislation on gun control.

● The first president to post his weekly address on YouTube
● The only president not born on the U.S. mainland (he was born in Hawaii)
● This president worked for Baskin-Robbins as a teenager

# Barack Obama

"For as much as government can do and must do, it is ultimately the faith and determination of the American people upon which this nation relies."

# Donald J. Trump
## 45th President  2017–incumbent

✳ This Republican was a real estate mogul and reality TV star
✳ His grandfather owned saloons in Seattle during the Gold Rush
✳ He has a star on the Hollywood Walk of Fame

When I was nominated, the Republican establishment went nuts. They thought the megawatt Trump name—though it glitters from casinos, luxury towers, and golf courses worldwide—would spell lights out on an election ballot. Bad call, wimps! I'm the Deal Maker Supreme, and my election was my big, big deal with history and the American people. I said what I thought and they liked it. The Donald became The President.

Now I'm in the Oval Office, working my comeback magic on the American economy. In the 1990s, my net worth took a major hit. For a while, I had to sell assets (my yacht!), live on a budget, and negotiate with creditors. But thanks to my signature swagger, I got mega rich again in just a few years! American debt, prepare to go bye bye!

● The first president to have a sister who is a federal judge
● The only president to appear on Wrestlemania (The Battle of the Billionaires)
● The only president to have been married three times

# Donald J. Trump

"My whole life is about winning."

# Portrait Gallery

So, you've read about America's chief executives, past and present. You know how they got to the top spot at the White House and what they did when they got there. Now it's time to get the bare facts as you make your way through the presidential portrait gallery.

**GEORGE WASHINGTON**
**Born:** February 22, 1732
  Westmoreland County,
  Virginia
**Died:** December 14, 1799
  Mount Vernon, Virginia
**Political Party:** None
**Vice President:** John Adams
  (1735–1826)
**First Lady:** Martha (Dandridge)
  Custis Washington
  (1731–1802)

**THOMAS JEFFERSON**
**Born:** April 13, 1743
  Shadwell, Virginia
**Died:** July 4, 1826
  Charlottesville, Virginia
**Political Party:** Democratic-
  Republican
**Vice Presidents:**
  Aaron Burr (1756–1836),
  George Clinton (1739–1812)
**First Lady:** None

**JOHN ADAMS**
**Born:** October 30, 1735
  Quincy, Massachusetts
**Died:** July 4, 1826
  Quincy, Massachusetts
**Political Party:** Federalist
**Vice President:** Thomas
  Jefferson (1743–1826)
**First Lady:** Abigail (Smith)
  Adams (1744–1818)

**JAMES MADISON**
**Born:** March 16, 1751
  Port Conway, Virginia
**Died:** June 28, 1836
  Montpelier, Virginia
**Political Party:** Democratic-
  Republican
**Vice Presidents:** George
  Clinton (1739–1812),
  Elbridge Gerry (1744–1814)
**First Lady:** Dolley (Payne)
  Todd Madison (1768–1849)

**JAMES MONROE**
**Born:** April 28, 1758
  Westmoreland County,
  Virginia
**Died:** July 4, 1831
  New York City, New York
**Political Party:** Democratic-
  Republican
**Vice President:** Daniel D.
  Tompkins (1774–1825)
**First Lady:** Elizabeth (Kortright)
  Monroe (1768–1830)

**MARTIN VAN BUREN**
**Born:** December 5, 1782
  Kinderhook, New York
**Died:** July 24, 1862
  Kinderhook, New York
**Political Party:** Democratic
**Vice President:** Richard M.
  Johnson (1780–1850)
**First Lady:** Angelica (Singleton)
  Van Buren (daughter-in-law,
  1818–1877)

**JOHN QUINCY ADAMS**
**Born:** July 11, 1767
  Quincy, Massachusetts
**Died:** February 23, 1848
  Washington, D.C.
**Political Party:** Democratic-
  Republican
**Vice President:** John C.
  Calhoun (1782–1850)
**First Lady:** Louisa
  (Johnson) Adams
  (1775–1852)

**WILLIAM HENRY HARRISON**
**Born:** February 9, 1773
  Charles City County, Virginia
**Died:** April 4, 1841
  Washington, D.C.
**Political Party:** Whig
**Vice President:** John Tyler
  (1790–1862)
**First Lady:** Anna (Symmes)
  Harrison (1775–1864)

**ANDREW JACKSON**
**Born:** March 15, 1767
  Waxhaws (North/
  South Carolina)
**Died:** June 8, 1845
  Nashville, Tennessee
**Political Party:** Democratic
**Vice Presidents:** John C.
  Calhoun (1782–1850),
  Martin Van Buren
  (1782–1862)
**First Lady:** Emily Donelson
  (niece, 1807–1836)

**JOHN TYLER**
**Born:** March 29, 1790
  Charles City County, Virginia
**Died:** January 18, 1862
  Richmond, Virginia
**Political Party:** Whig/
  Independent
**Vice President:** None
**First Ladies:** Letitia (Christian)
  Tyler (1790–1842), Julia
  (Gardiner) Tyler (1820–1889)

### JAMES K. POLK
**Born:** November 2, 1795
Pineville, North Carolina
**Died:** June 15, 1849
Nashville, Tennessee
**Political Party:** Democratic
**Vice President:** George M.
Dallas (1792–1864)
**First Lady:** Sarah (Childress)
Polk (1803–1891)

### FRANKLIN PIERCE
**Born:** November 23, 1804
Hillsborough, New Hampshire
**Died:** October 8, 1869
Concord, New Hampshire
**Political Party:** Democratic
**Vice President:** William R. King
(1786–1853)
**First Lady:** Jane (Appleton)
Pierce (1806–1863)

### ZACHARY TAYLOR
**Born:** November 24, 1784
Barboursville, Virginia
**Died:** July 9, 1850
Washington, D.C.
**Political Party:** Whig
**Vice President:** Millard
Fillmore (1800–1874)
**First Lady:** Margaret (Smith)
Taylor (1788–1852)

### JAMES BUCHANAN
**Born:** April 32, 1791
Cove Gap, Pennsylvania
**Died:** June 1, 1868
Lancaster, Pennsylvania
**Political Party:** Democratic
**Vice President:** John C.
Breckinridge (1821–1875)
**First Lady:** Harriet Lane
(niece, 1830–1903)

### MILLARD FILLMORE
**Born:** January 7, 1800
Summerhill, New York
**Died:** March 8, 1874
Buffalo, New York
**Political Party:** Whig
**Vice President:** None
**First Lady:** Abigail (Powers)
Fillmore (1798–1853)

### ABRAHAM LINCOLN
**Born:** February 12, 1809
Hodgenville, Kentucky
**Died:** April 15, 1865
Washington, D.C.
**Political Party:** Republican
**Vice Presidents:** Hannibal
Hamlin (1809–1891),
Andrew Johnson
(1808–1875)
**First Lady:** Mary (Todd) Lincoln
(1818–1882)

**ANDREW JOHNSON**
**Born:** December 29, 1808
Raleigh, North Carolina
**Died:** July 31, 1875
Elizabethton, Tennessee
**Political Party:** Democratic
**Vice President:** None
**First Lady:** Eliza (McCardle)
Johnson (1810–1876)

**JAMES A. GARFIELD**
**Born:** November 19, 1831
Moreland Hills, Ohio
**Died:** September 19, 1881
Elberon, New Jersey
**Political Party:** Republican
**Vice President:** Chester A.
Arthur (1829–1886)
**First Lady:** Lucretia (Rudolph)
Garfield (1832–1918)

**ULYSSES S. GRANT**
**Born:** April 27, 1822
Point Pleasant, Ohio
**Died:** July 23, 1885
Wilton, New York
**Political Party:** Republican
**Vice Presidents:** Schuyler
Colfax (1823–1885),
Henry Wilson (1812–1875)
**First Lady:** Julia (Dent)
Grant (1826–1902)

**CHESTER A. ARTHUR**
**Born:** October 5, 1829
Fairfield, Vermont
**Died:** November 18, 1886
New York City, New York
**Political Party:** Republican
**Vice President:** None
**First Lady:** None

**RUTHERFORD B. HAYES**
**Born:** October 4, 1822
Delaware, Ohio
**Died:** January 17, 1893
Fremont, Ohio
**Political Party:** Republican
**Vice President:** William A.
Wheeler (1819–1887)
**First Lady:** Lucy (Webb)
Hayes (1831–1889)

**GROVER CLEVELAND**
**Born:** March 18, 1837
Caldwell, New Jersey
**Died:** June 24, 1908
Princeton, New Jersey
**Political Party:** Democratic
**Vice Presidents:** Thomas A.
Hendricks (1819–1885),
Adlai E. Stevenson I
(1835–1914)
**First Lady:** Frances (Folsom)
Cleveland (1864–1947)

**BENJAMIN HARRISON**
**Born:** August 20, 1833
North Bend, Ohio
**Died:** March 13, 1901
Indianapolis, Indiana
**Political Party:** Republican
**Vice President:** Levi P. Morton
(1824–1920)
**First Lady:** Caroline (Scott)
Harrison (1832–1892)

**WILLIAM HOWARD TAFT**
**Born:** September 15, 1857
Cincinnati, Ohio
**Died:** March 8, 1930
Washington, D.C.
**Political Party:** Republican
**Vice President:** James S.
Sherman (1855–1912)
**First Lady:** Helen (Herron) Taft
(1861–1943)

**WILLIAM MCKINLEY**
**Born:** January 29, 1843
Niles, Ohio
**Died:** September 14, 1901
Buffalo, New York
**Political Party:** Republican
**Vice Presidents:** Garret A.
Hobart (1844–1899),
Theodore Roosevelt
(1858–1919)
**First Lady:** Ida (Saxton)
McKinley (1847–1907)

**WOODROW WILSON**
**Born:** December 28, 1856
Staunton, Virginia
**Died:** February 3, 1924
Washington, D.C.
**Political Party:** Democratic
**Vice President:** Thomas R.
Marshall (1854–1925)
**First Ladies:** Ellen (Axson) Wilson
(1860–1914), Edith (Bolling)
Galt Wilson (1872–1961)

**THEODORE ROOSEVELT**
**Born:** October 27, 1858
New York City, New York
**Died:** January 6, 1919
Oyster Bay, New York
**Political Party:** Republican
**Vice President:** Charles W.
Fairbanks (1852–1918)
**First Lady:** Edith (Carow)
Roosevelt (1861–1948)

**WARREN G. HARDING**
**Born:** November 2, 1865
Blooming Grove, Ohio
**Died:** August 2, 1923
San Francisco, California
**Political Party:** Republican
**Vice President:** Calvin
Coolidge (1872–1933)
**First Lady:** Florence (Kling)
Harding (1860–1924)

## CALVIN COOLIDGE

**Born:** July 4, 1872
  Plymouth, Vermont
**Died:** January 5, 1933
  Northampton, Massachusetts
**Political Party:** Republican
**Vice President:** Charles G.
  Dawes (1865–1951)
**First Lady:** Grace (Goodhue)
  Coolidge (1879–1957)

## HARRY S. TRUMAN

**Born:** May 8, 1884
  Lamar, Missouri
**Died:** December 26, 1972
  Kansas City, Missouri
**Political Party:** Democratic
**Vice President:** Alben W.
  Barkley (1877–1956)
**First Lady:** Bess      (Wallace)
  Truman (1885–1982)

## HERBERT HOOVER

**Born:** August 10, 1874
  West Branch, Iowa
**Died:** October 20, 1964
  New York City, New York
**Political Party:** Republican
**Vice President:** Charles Curtis
  (1860–1936)
**First Lady:** Lou (Henry) Hoover
  (1874–1944)

## DWIGHT D. EISENHOWER

**Born:** October 14, 1890
  Denison, Texas
**Died:** March 28, 1969
  Washington, D.C.
**Political Party:** Republican
**Vice President:** Richard
  Nixon (1913–1994)
**First Lady:** Mamie (Doud)
  Eisenhower (1896–1979)

## FRANKLIN D. ROOSEVELT

**Born:** January 30, 1882
  Hyde Park, New York
**Died:** April 12, 1945
  Warm Springs, Georgia
**Political Party:** Democratic
**Vice Presidents:** John N.
  Garner (1868–1967),
  Henry A. Wallace
  (1888–1965), Harry S.
  Truman (1884–1972)
**First Lady:** Eleanor (Roosevelt)
  Roosevelt (1884–1962)

## JOHN F. KENNEDY

**Born:** May 29, 1917
  Brookline, Massachusetts
**Died:** November 22, 1963
  Dallas, Texas
**Political Party**: Democratic
**Vice President:** Lyndon B.
  Johnson (1908–1973)
**First Lady:** Jacqueline
  (Bouvier) Kennedy
  (1929–1994)

### LYNDON B. JOHNSON

**Born:** August 27, 1908
  Stonewall, Texas
**Died:** January 22, 1973
  Stonewall, Texas
**Political Party:** Democratic
**Vice President:** Hubert
  Humphrey (1911–1978)
**First Lady:** Claudia "Lady Bird"
  (Taylor) Johnson (1912–2007)

### JIMMY CARTER

**Born:** October 1, 1924
  Plains, Georgia
**Political Party:** Democratic
**Vice President:** Walter Mondale
  (b. 1928)
**First Lady:** Rosalynn (Smith)
  Carter (b. 1927)

### RICHARD NIXON

**Born:** January 9, 1913
  Yorba Linda, California
**Died:** April 22, 1994
  New York City, New York
**Political Party:** Republican
**Vice Presidents:** Spiro T.
  Agnew (1918–1996),
  Gerald Ford (1913–2006)
**First Lady:** Patricia (Ryan)
  Nixon (1912–1993)

### RONALD REAGAN

**Born:** February 6, 1911
  Tampico, Illinois
**Died:** June 5, 2004
  Los Angeles, California
**Political Party:** Republican
**Vice President:** George H. W.
  Bush (b. 1924)
**First Lady:** Nancy (Davis)
  Reagan (1921–2016)

### GERALD FORD

**Born:** July 14, 1913
  Omaha, Nebraska
**Died:** December 26, 2006
  Rancho Mirage, California
**Political Party:** Republican
**Vice President:** Nelson
  Rockefeller (1908–1979)
**First Lady:** Betty (Bloomer)
  Warren Ford (1918–2011)

### GEORGE H. W. BUSH

**Born:** June 12, 1924
  Milton, Massachusetts
**Political Party:** Republican
**Vice President:** Dan Quayle
  (b. 1947)
**First Lady:** Barbara (Pierce)
  Bush (b. 1925)

**BILL CLINTON**
**Born:** August 19, 1946
Hope, Arkansas
**Political Party:** Democratic
**Vice President:** Al Gore
(b. 1948)
**First Lady:** Hillary (Rodham)
Clinton (b. 1947)

**DONALD J. TRUMP**
**Born:** June 14, 1946
Queens, New York City
**Political Party:** Republican
**Vice President:** Mike Pence
(b. 1959)
**First Lady:** Melania (Knauss)
Trump (b. 1970)

**GEORGE W. BUSH**
**Born:** July 6, 1946
New Haven, Connecticut
**Political Party:** Republican
**Vice President:** Dick Cheney
(b. 1941)
**First Lady:** Laura (Welch) Bush
(b. 1946)

**BARACK OBAMA**
**Born:** August 4, 1961
Honolulu, Hawaii
**Political Party:** Democratic
**Vice President:** Joe Biden
(b. 1942)
**First Lady:** Michelle (Robinson)
Obama (b. 1964)

# Glossary

**Acquit** To clear a person from a charge or accusation.
**Amendment** A formal change to the U.S. Constitution, added to the end in a separate section of writing.
**Annex** To add territory to a country, often by military force.
**Bill** A version of a new law that is proposed and debated in Congress.
**Bill of Rights** The first ten amendments to the Constitution. They guarantee the civil rights of U.S. citizens.
**Cabinet** The team that helps the president do his job, usually heads of federal departments and agencies.
**Civil rights** The rights of all citizens to freedom and equality.
**Civil service** The federal government departments that are not part of the military.
**Confederacy** The 11 Southern states that left the United States in 1860–1861 to form a separate country.
**Congress** The group that makes U.S. laws, composed of the House of Representatives and the Senate.
**Constitution** The text that sets out how the U.S. government is organized. It was adopted in 1787.
**Declaration of Independence** A text drafted in 1776 by Thomas Jefferson and signed by representatives of the 13 colonies, declaring that the United States was independent of Great Britain.
**Democratic Party** One of the two main U.S. political parties. It began in 1828 and favors progressive policies and programs that help ordinary people.

**Democratic-Republican Party** A political party that came before the modern Democratic Party. Founded in 1792 by Thomas Jefferson, it opposed a strong national government.

**Depression** A period in which the economy is in bad shape and many people have little money.

**Electoral College** A group of people that vote on behalf of the states for the election of the president and vice president. A vote cast by an Electoral College member is called an electoral vote.

**Electorate** Those who are allowed to vote in a country.

**Emancipation** The granting of freedom from slavery.

**Federal** A system of government in which several states combine to make a country, but each state has some power to govern itself. Anything relating to the United States as a whole (rather than individual states) is a federal issue—for example, foreign policy, security, and postage.

**Federalist Party** An early political party, founded in 1787, that favored a strong central government.

**Fraud** A crime that usually involves lying and cheating in order to get money or property.

**Freedmen** Former slaves who were emancipated.

**Front-porch campaign** An election campaign in which the presidential candidate doesn't travel around much. James A. Garfield (1880), Benjamin Harrison (1888), and William McKinley (1896) ran front-porch campaigns.

**House of Representatives** The lower house of Congress. Each state is represented in the House according to its population.

**Impeach** To accuse an important elected official, such as the president, of a crime connected with their job. The process is called impeachment.

**Inauguration** The ceremony that makes a new president official. The president usually gives a speech about their plans for the nation.

**Manifest Destiny** A 19th-Century idea that the United States must expand all the way to the Pacific Ocean.

**National debt** The amount of money that a country's government has borrowed and must one day pay back.

**NATO** A group of 28 nations (including the United States, Canada, and certain European countries), where each one agrees to defend any other if one of them is attacked. NATO stands for North Atlantic Treaty Organization.

**Party politics** Arguing and name-calling between parties with the aim of making the other party look bad or wrong.

**Pentagon** The headquarters of the United States Department of Defense.

**Polling** The voting process in an election.

**Progressive policies** Policies that favor good living conditions for all people and the ability of everyone to enjoy the same opportunities.

**Reconstruction Era** The period (1865–1877) following the Civil War when the former states of the Confederacy were governed by the federal government.

**Republican Party** One of the two main U.S. political parties. It favors lower taxes and less government control over businesses. It was founded in 1854.

**Secede** When a state secedes, it formally leaves the group that it belongs to; 11 Southern states seceded from the United States in 1860–1861.

**Segregation** The separation of people into racial groups in daily life, for activities such as traveling on public transportation and eating in restaurants.

**Senate** The upper house of Congress. The Senate is smaller than the House of Representatives because just two Senators represent each state.

**Separation of powers** A model of government that splits the government into executive (president), legislative (Congress), and judicial (Supreme Court) branches. A system of "checks and balances" makes sure that no branch has more power than the others.

**Union** All of the different U.S. states considered as one. During the Civil War, "Union" described the 20 free states and five border states that did not join the Confederacy.

**Veto** A decision by the president not to sign a bill passed by the Congress. This makes it harder for the bill to become a law.

**Whig Party** A party formed in 1834 by some former members of the Democratic-Republican Party. This party came before the Republican Party and dissolved in 1854.

**White supremacist** Someone who believes (mistakenly) that white people are superior to all other races.

# Index

President entries in **bold**